The Breakfast Egg

Maria Cura

The Breakfast Egg

How the Dependencies of the World are reflected in an Egg

The little Book

This little book is an excerpt from the German book "Geschenk Lebenssinn" by Maria Cura.

Bibliographic information of the
Deutsche Nationalbibliothek:
The Deutsche Nationalbibliothek records this
publication in the Deutsche Nationalbibliografie;
detailed bibliographic data are available on the
Internet at: http://dnb.dnb.de.

© Januar Maria Cura
Production and publisher (Herstellung und
Verlag): BoD - Books on Demand, Norderstedt
ISBN: 9783748192879

Cover image: Maria Cura

Grateful to the chickens,
who have been giving
tasteful eggs
to us
since ancient times

Content

About my Translation

Since I do not have the opportunity to hire a professional translator, I try to translate this little book by myself.

So if something seems unusual to you - please be lenient - I am doing my very best.

What is meant to be said in this little book can be understood even if some passages should be not quite clear. But I am optimistic, that everything is understandable.

Foreword

The breakfast egg, which was eaten 100 or 50 years ago, looked just like today and probably tasted about as we know it.

But the way and the environment, in which the egg was laid, transported and sold is now completely different to the old times. But the issue here in the book is not the well known theme of animal protection.

Rather, it is about dependencies that all play a role until the egg can be consumed by us. These dependencies have dramatically increased over the last 50 years. Dependencies are not only found in the process of laying eggs, transporting and selling them, but they also can be found in many other areas and these areas are widely ramified. If, as happened here, one tries to sum up the dependencies, then a surprisingly long "litany" comes about.

The egg (and its environment), that served as a breakfast egg 50 years ago I confront with an egg from a great chicken farm of today (2017). It may be that the list of dependencies is not complete, or the one or other point is not necessary (e.g., robots for packaging). The point here is not to provide an exact instruction for the construction and operation of an chicken farm. But the general impression, that comes up by reading the following text, shows typically, in how many aspects most of the products we consume are dependent, how many areas all must function and work together, until that the product can finally be acquired by us in the usual way. Very often, when we are consumers, we do not realize the many dependencies.

The breakfast egg is just an example. The same applies to most modern products, they all stand in countless dependencies: be it a shampoo, a piece of furniture, a smart phone, a watch, a computer program, a piece of clothing and so on and so on.

The list of dependencies on the example of the breakfast egg first was published in the book "Geschenk Lebenssinn" (English: "The Gift of the Meaning of Life"), which contains even more themes of thoughtful, cultural-critical considerations about different topics.

Maria Cura, Munich in October 2017 (German version) and January 2019 (English version)

How was it on a Farm 50 Years ago?

Before 100 and often even only 50 years ago, many small farms had their own chickens, these were running around cheerfully in the yard, guarded by a proud cock. The farmers were able to produce the hen house themselves, the chickens were fed with food from their own farming or at least from the surrounding area, and these chickens were also able to look for food on their own, scratching the ground.

The farmer kept the hen house in order and collected the eggs which were consumed by the family and the farmhands, or sold to the townspeople in the neighborhood. Perhaps there were already small corner shops, which regularly bought a few eggs from the nearby farmers.

The chickens were domesticated, but they still lived a fairly natural life; they had a cock in their midst to match their natural needs, and they were allowed to hatch and raise chicks as offspring. They did not even needed to be put inside a fence, they stayed voluntarily close to the house. And early in the morning, at sunrise, the cock waked the peasant´s family up if it was perhaps still sleeping (and the cock was not sentenced at court for being disturbing nervous neighbors). The life of the rural population was mostly very hard, this is not to be romanticized here, but it was manifold and at the same time readily comprehensible.

It is also worth mentioning, that there are firms in the eco-movement, that keep chickens as natural as possible, which is very positive. But these farms are also now far more dependent on many more things than the farmers in old times, as social structures and the economy have changed a lot. Nobody can escape this today, who is not completely self-sufficient and lives as a hermit.

I think the multifaceted interwoven dependencies of the production of goods are something that concerns all of us, because these dependencies create new possibilities as well as new restrictions. Only when we consciously understand this, we can decide how we want to shape our social and cultural future.

It is already the sheer sum of today's dependencies, which is surprising when one begins to deal with it. Let yourself be invited on the following pages to an astonishing journey through the dependencies of a simple modern breakfast egg.

The Dependencies in which our Breakfast Egg (from the Supermarket) stands today

What has to become our breakfast egg, must be laid as an egg by a hen.

Hens are bred beforehand in extra farms. There are probably extra **rooms for hatchery**, where the right temperature prevails for incubation. A modern **heating system** with regulation and **monitoring** ensures even temperature, perhaps also humidity. Possibly the **eggs have to be moved**. The chicks must be fed with the **right food**. Male chickens are sorted out. Soon, the chicks are **packed in boxes** and driven to the chicken farms with suitable **trucks**. There they are presumably kept in their age group, separate from the other hens.

Here too, in the Lefabrik, the **conditions are closely monitored and regulated**. The **feed is precisely calculated in its composition**. For example, So that the egg yolk becomes darker yellow or lighter, depending on the wish and buyer behavior. Water must be available. The **eggs roll away** from the hen **into the catchers**, are **sorted and packed according to size**.

The hens, which live so densely, tend to **disease**. To ensure that they do not infect each other too much, they are closely monitored, and the **veterinarian** is coming regularly. In the smallest suspicion hens are sorted out or **drugs, also antibiotics** given. If there is an **epidemic danger**, detailed investigations must be carried out and, if suspected, bird flu, all animals are killed.

The **manure** is highly concentrated and has to be **specially disposed** of in these large quantities. Perhaps there is an own company that does this.

But before this can happen, the **building** for the hens has to be built - with or without free space -, preferably with an **office, a technical room for heating** and other necessary regulators, a place, where the laid eggs are collected, a **room for sorting and a control room**. Eggs get packed in a **packing room**, where the **egg cartons - previously produced in a different place and then delivered** - get filled with the right number of eggs and get provided with a durability **date**. They get packed to large package units, stored for a short time in a **storage room, loaded with forklift into**

trucks and sent on a certain route. Other eggs may be refrigerated or delivered to other companies for egg products. Broken eggs must be disposed of well. **Hygiene regulations** must be strictly adhered to, **disinfectants** are presumably used in great amount..

But we are still talking about the **building**, which is not standing yet at all. A **building ground must be found** and it has to be hoped that the population does not protest too much. An **architect (with education at the university)** and a specialized **technician** create a construction plan, make **cost estimates**, get **offers**, hold **meetings**. The **municipality and the supervisory authorities** must agree.

The **investor**, possibly a stock company, is now convinced that this will be a profitable project. His planner has set up a **financial plan** with all costs. The possibility to set some of the cost off against tax liability was of course taken into account.

When everything has been accepted (perhaps with intermediate obstacles of civil protests and the involvement of **lawyers**), the **heavy construction vehicles** (which also were developed and built) and **building materials** appear. Perhaps they will also be building **a street to the building and a parking lot** for the later coming trucks.

After completion of the building comes the first delivery of the young hens. Now the machinery is running, it can start soon. An experienced chicken farm **Master supervises everything**. The **technician** checks all technical procedures, if something does not work (for example, heater heats too strongly, feed-flow tape is blocked), he takes care, that soon everything is working again, because he has the professional qualification for this. The **logistic engineer plans the process with the trucks**, so that all the eggs go to the supermarket where they were ordered (whether Easter is particularly difficult?).

Without **water**, hens don´t live long. Therefore clean water must be provided. But even employees must be able to **wash** themselves, the **toilets** should work. The **water comes through pipes from sources, depths or cleared from rivers**. The **water industry** is itself again a large area, which must also work, so that the hens lay their eggs. There must be **waterworks** - and, of course, **sewage treatment plants, garbage disposal, garbage processing**. And if we are already talking about the cleanliness, we should also not forget the

cleaning staff and the production of **cleaning agents**.

Electricity works (as we have already learned in the Monopoly game as children) must also be available, and with also (in the Monopoly game not necessary) **electricity storage and electricity routes**, as well as **generating electricity** (**nuclear power with disposal problems, now more wind turbines, solar energy, hydropower**, etc.). These techniques are also a world of their own and also from them the egg-laying hens are dependent).

Long before the beginning of the production, the **marketing department** has written to the supermarkets and other large distributors, and advertised to offer their products. Some markets want their own **label**, which has to be designed and manufactured by the **graphic artist**. The **cartons** are manufactured in a factory specialized in the latter with the appropriate labels. For this, the **quantities have to be calculated** so that a reasonable volume discount can be negotiated and the bearing does not have to be too large.

In a large chicken farm the **eggs are probably measured by the robot, stamped and then sorted into cartons according to their size**, or they are used for other purposes than selling in the supermarket. Perhaps the eggs will also be lit with special light to **sort out defective or bad eggs** - all **fully automatic.**

The data on the quantities of the eggs produced and packed according to size are entered into the **book-keeping** as soon as the **barcode** is **registered**. When they are sold, they are again registered in the accounting system as outgoing goods, **accounting software** makes it easy to book huge quantities. The **invoices** are also **created with a fast program**, with discount and delivery costs and VAT. An **enveloping machine** does everything else. Then the bills go to the **post office**.

Arrival and departure of the **truck drivers** are exactly coordinated, the trucks come at the right time, pick up the right quantity and drive it to the customers on precisely planned routes in an optimal short time. **Large packs are welded up by robots**, they make the delivery of large quantities easier.

Once a year, there is an **stock-taking**, and once a year a **tax declaration** is given. For this purpose, a competent **tax consultant** is employed, who can use his **knowledge acquired during his studies**.

But studying alone is not enough, new tax laws and additions to the old ones are constantly enacted, **he has to develop continuously**, if he wants to get the best out of the company.

The **marketing department** must always try to **reach all possible customers (especially wholesalers and supermarkets)**. For this, they need **addresses**, there are companies where you can buy addresses. Potential customers with whom there is already existing a contact, must be stored with their data in an **address database**, the **data have to be maintained** and updated. The marketing department tries to win customers, who are still buying eggs from other companies, with regular special offers and actions. Customers are invited personally by **trade representatives**. In addition, once and again new **eyecatchers** should appear on the label. The other companies with their marketing strategies are closely monitored, as well as the customers: do they prefer a colorful label, or a simple, ecologically looking one? Should chickens be pictured on the meadow?

It is not an expression of pure greed. Companies who do not take part in the competition will soon have to close their company, because the customer quickly moved to another supplier.

Without cartons no eggs are sold, and there is no effective advertising without the glued-on printed paper. **For cardboard and paper**, **trees** have to grow, be felled and **transported**, in **paper factories** the wood gets **processed** and then **sold**. Or **waste paper** is **collected** and recycled. At any rate **without paper or cardboard no egg containers**, but also **no invoice** (exception: if the invoice is electronically - but for the financial office electronic invoices are perhaps not sufficient), **no contracts**. In nature, where the trees have been beaten, must be **reforested**, and nature conservation is worried internationally about too much and too fast **deforestation**. Loss of forests locally or **globally affects the climate**.

To bring the company also well on the Internet, a **website** is designed and an **SEO company is commissioned** to ensure that this website is found by the search engines, especially Google, and If possible, on page 1. This requires **experts** who have the **knowledge how the algorithms of the Google search function are working** (but these algorithms are changing once and again).

A lot of things are done by **computer**. These have been **developed** by completely different companies and are nevertheless indispensable for a modern large fab factory.

Computers and robots have already worked for the production of these computers, because much of the technology is so small and complicated that humans alone can no longer manufacture it. For the **hardware**, some **rare earths** are used, elements that are rarely found in a few areas of the earth. There they have to be **discovered and digged up**. Here, too, the **political situation in countries of occurrence of these elements** is significant and also the **customs laws**. The **manufacturers of the computer elements or the necessary materials** try to buy the raw materials in the countries where they are sold as cheaply as possible. Under what conditions these rare earths, and whether environmentally friendly or not, are won, that is generally not known so well. It may also be, that no one wants to know it exactly, how the elements come into our computers. **Recycling companies** are also involved here in order to recover the precious raw materials (and these recycling companies are dependent on consumers who bring their computers to the recycling yard). Perhaps the Breakfast Egg AG (name invented by me, does not refer to any real egg producer) transacts a lot of the data over an **IT-cloud** - then they need somewhere in the world connection to **huge storage units**. All this is **necessary so that the egg factory can control, calculate, logistically plan, but also pay salaries and much more.**

But the computers do not only need hardware, even generations of **IT specialists have developed computer languages and programmed programs,** They have sold or placed in the cloud. Because of the **data security** many IT data security experts are added to the IT-specialists.

At least one **bank** needs the Breakfast Eggs AG. The AG probably **raised credits**, and also had to transfer money to a bank. It had to pay the expenses and salaries there and pay hits taxes through the bank account. However, the Breakfast Eggs AG has **not only contact with its bank, but also with the banks of its customers**. And of course there must be money, real or virtual, the **financial policies of the states** and the **international exchange rates** as well as the **interest rate policy** play a role.

The whole **banking system** and the **stock market** with its speculations and stock exchange courses is **linked to the Breakfast Eggs AG**. Shares of Breakfast Eggs AG can be purchased or sold worldwide. **Shareholders 'meetings** must be held, **stock prices** should be **watched**, **shareholders' profits** should be good, so that the shareholder are kept in good mood - otherwise it would soon be the end of laying eggs in the Breakfast Eggs AG.

Other **competing companies** and their prices are **observed** and have an important role. Perhaps one secretly makes price agreements. **Trade agreements** such as the planned but controversial TTIP could have an impact (e.g, for the feed industry).

The **managers** of the Breakfast Eggs AG have to travel a lot to get to **meetings**, to attend training courses, to learn new techniques and to learn of other companies who offer chicks abroad. And, of course, they have to supervise the numerous own farms. They usually do not have much time and often **need an airplane**. So the **world of flying** (with the production of airplanes, fuel, pilots, training, flight personnel, food supplies, airports, trade unions, etc.) therefore is also in connection with the Breakfast Eggs AG.

And almost I would have forgotten the **smartphones** and the **telephone system.**

The Breakfast Eggs AG has, if the company is big

enough, **union representatives** and a **works council**.

In the EU often **new laws** are passed for food production and agriculture. There must be **experts, lawyers, commissions** (and probably many **lobbyists**). The new laws must be presented, adopted and published. All these experts and lawyers have **studied** well and have acquired knowledge for a long time. For them **Universities were entertained, books were printed, seminars were held**.

The same applies to the **veterinarians** (now we are again closer to the hens). After getting the high-school diploma, they had to study for a long time and are still being trained today (by the pharmaceutical industry?). Without these possibilities of study, there would not be doctors who know what diseases there are among the chickens, how dangerous they are, which drugs can help, or when the animals have to be slaughtered.

The **knowledge of the feed-manufacturers** is as well very considerable. They also have to look, **from which country, from which supplier** they buy **whatever ingredients** at what price and in which quality. Presumably there are used **global trade relationships** - it is very well possible that components from all continents come together in one fodder. Not only nutritious grains are fed, but there are **additions of minerals, vitamins, medicines, substances that affect the color of the yolk, presumably also hormones and probably even more**. Where these substances are produced is also determined by the price, and the offers can come from various countries (e.g., India). There will be a **quality control**, whether it is reliable, I do not know. At any rate, without this industry, most propabely it would not be possible to fed the hens in today's giant factory plants. And most importantly, the hens would not be able to get new eggs quickly enough.

Many **farmers who cultivate forage** are likely to need **pesticides, insecticides, fungicides and many fertilizers** (other than organic farming) that **have been** and are being **developed.** For these also **raw materials are needed**, that have been acquired or need to be produced and marketed. **Genetic research** provides **new seeds** and the seed rights must also be monitored and controlled.

Since some **components of the feed** (but also the required trucks, computers, etc.) **come from overseas or Asia, container ships, large ports and trained captains** are necessary. How many things, people, plans, laws, etc., are needed again for shipping, I do not even want to start to to try to list them.

The **policy and the health office** must or should at least ensure that no things are used at the Breakfast Eggs AG, that are harmful to human health. **Animal welfare** issues must also be taken into account. **Hygiene regulations** must be enacted and reviewed. On the consumer side, institutes are investigating **cholesterol** (eggs contain much cholesterol) and other food ingredients, giving **nutritional advice** to physicians and consumers. The discussion about the harmfulness of cholesterol (which is now partially questioned again) has an influence on the purchasing behavior of the eggs consumers.

The **pharmaceutical industry** must always develop and **test new antibiotics** in **research laboratories** (because the old ones become ineffective because of the resistances) (for this purpose, computer programs are necessary for evaluation). The **approval** can be achieved **in complex approval procedures**. The state would have to monitor the activities of the pharmaceutical industry. Since too many antibiotics are used, the state is called upon to impose restrictive laws. These must then be checked again for their compliance. Through **seminars** and marketing veterinarians are informed about new means. The **journalism** can write about the **antibiotic consumption in the chicken farm** and thereby trigger **protests**.

Without the **truck drivers** would not come eggs of the Breakfast Eggs AG to the consumers. The **trucks have to be built and bought**. They consist of many parts (**tires, engines, cooling, brakes, housings, computers**, etc.), everything has to be **developed, tested, probed** and **production lines with robots** are built and so on. The drivers learn to drive these large transportation weighs (truck driver's license), they need a job with a contract. There are **regulations on driving time** and presumably also other laws. Without **roads** and without **traffic regulations** no egg would enter the supermarket: therefore **road construction and traffic guard** are necessary. Likewise is the **fuel**, the diesel, an important factor - without fuel the eggs would rotten in great numbers within the chicken farm. So **oil** has to be **pumped up** in the countries where it occurs, it must be **refined** and needs to **be brought to the service stations in Germany** (of course there must be a sufficient gas stations).

The **tax offices** must deal with the tax declaration of the Breakfast Eggs AG and make a **tax assessment**. The **VAT** paid to the suppliers has to be refund (the task of the politics are to issue the **tax laws**).

To let people know which dishes can be cooked with eggs (not only breakfast eggs), **cookery books** are written, are offered and sold in bookshops. Also in **chefkoch.de** and on other websites more and more recipes are collected and evaluated.

Some people need an **egg cooker** to cook eggs - the egg cooker also must be developed, produced (with the necessary materials) and sold. But most people will use a **modern stove**, with a suitable **pot**.

Without **current** there are no eggs in the chicken farm nothing works without electricity, most of the technology would stand still, the hens would probably perish miserably , But also no computer, no telephone would work more. And at home with the electric cooker there would be no boiling water on the electric stove, with which the egg could be cooked, also roasts in the pan would not be possible. However, some consumers use a gas stove and are dependent on the **gas**.

The **employees** at Breakfast Egg AG may **need cars** (and therefore petrol, oil, batteries) to get to work, and the **mothers or fathers are looking for a day care center** for their children. Cars and kindergartens must also be produced or operated. **Laws for cars and about the places in the kindergartens** regulate many things, **kindergarteners are trained**, meals (also with eggs) are to be wholesome but cheaply in the kiosks and kindergartens.

To offer the eggs to the end user there must be **supermarket chains** (or on-line delivery services). What is connected with this again, until a supermarket chain can exist - I do not think that I need to explain that now. Oh, the shopping bag is also necessary.

And everything is now there: and the egg cooks in the morning on the stove and is soon placed in an **egg cup** and consumed with pleasure or in haste by us. Is not that a simple world? We consumers do not need to go every day to the hen house, collect the eggs, look after the chickens, feed them, keep the barn clean and maybe repair it. In extreme cases we can call a delivery service and the eggs are simply delivered to the door, the egg cooker takes over the cooking - everything quite simply. Or not?

By the way, eggs still form in the body of hens, of birds, and the eggs, which contained living growing chicks inside, had originally the task to pass on the lives of the parent animals and preserve the species. I am not a vegetarian and like eggs, but now and then I like to remember where our food comes from, I remember it with respect and gratitude. And we human beings and the chickens, we have been colonizing this planet for millions of years together. Humans and chickens were managing their survival independently without technology and were living this way through the millennia to today.

That an investor for giant chicken farms perhaps today the chicken, With all the described dependencies, quickly considered as a side issue that must work - this is actually no longer amazing.

Epilogue

Some readers may find the frequency of bold terms in the main text unusual or perhaps even disturbing. However, I have come to the conclusion that this design reflects visually exactly the situation of the many aspects to be considered in an egg factory, because many of these aspects are not organically and vividly connected (as a liquid typeface would suggest). The connecting parenthesis consists mainly of the computational profit of the company. The company is probably virtually supported by a computer program. For this purpose, the aspects to be considered are broken down into abstracted positions and numerical values.

The chicken interests big companies only as far as it produces goods, that means eggs. The consumer is only of interest for the companies in the the way he spends money, so whether and how much eggs he buys. Almost all other factors are only aids of technical nature, are artificial control by feed and drug selection, necessary planned marketing or rules and laws. That is why the individual elements necessary for production and sale no longer develop a very lively relationship. Correspondingly, the bold-printed words are in this booklet, like staccato-like points in a project plan.

On the old farmstead, on the other hand, the connection was much closer and livelier - between chickens, who were personally fed from the farmers and on the other hand the farmers' family, who liked to eat the fresh eggs of their chickens. This is also reflected in the quieter, more fluent character of the writing, which was quite natural in the chapter on the old farms.

For your own thoughts

For your own thoughts